PAINTED
LADIES

PAINTED LADIES

The art of hand-colouring in photography

JAMES WEDGE

Dragon's World Ltd.
Limpsfield
Surrey RH8 0DY
Great Britain

First published by Dragon's World 1988
© Dragon's World 1988
© James Wedge 1988
© Step-by-step illustrations by Will Giles and
Sandra Pond

Editorial   Phil Wilkinson
Design   Bob Gordon

British Library Cataloguing in Publication Data
Wedge, James
    Painted ladies: the art of hand colouring
    in photography.
    1. Photographs. Hand colouring
    I. Title
    778.8

ISBN Hardback 1 85028 055 X
        Limpback 1 85028 056 8

Typeset by Florencetype Ltd., Kewstoke, Avon
Printed in Singapore

HALF-TITLE PAGE PICTURE
For this lingerie picture for *19* magazine, I decided
to use an old house that I had photographed some
years before for *Interiors*. I love to use old and
unmodernized buildings for photography. They
are full of character, with textures on their
surfaces that only time can create. When we shot
this picture it was a freezing cold day. With no
heating in the building it needed a good
professional model to pose so naturally wearing so
little clothing. Out of shot, our team were
standing in full-length overcoats, scarves, and
gloves, stamping our feet. I used minimal colour
on this picture, since I felt that strong colour
would have spoilt the atmosphere.

| **Camera** Contax |
| **Film** Tri-X |
| **Print** Bromide |
| **Colour application** Paintbrush |

TITLE PAGE PICTURE
This picture was shot on location in Jersey. I
wanted a colour picture, but without too much
colour, so I decided to use hand-tinting. After
printing the picture in the normal way, I dyed the
print in a bath of shirt dye, which I had mixed to
make a parchment colour. I lightly tinted the print
after it had dried.

| **Camera** Canon |
| **Film** Tri-X |
| **Print** Bromide |
| **Colour application** Dyeing, paintbrush, airbrush, and cotton wool |

CONTENTS

INTRODUCTION
BY ADRIAN BAILEY

The hand-colouring of prints is an art almost as old as photography itself. The first attempts were made in 1843 by the assistants of William Henry Fox Talbot, who applied water colours to the matt-surface "Calotype" paper used to make prints from the negatives. It was, of course, Fox Talbot who invented and patented the negative-positive process. Some progress was also made in colouring Daguerreotypes, but with less success, since the image was made up of minute globules of mercury adhering to a metal plate, sealed under glass. The colourist had to apply powder colours with a fine brush, or colours with alcohol.

Then, in 1851, came Frederick Scott Archer's collodion process and his Ambrotype – a positive image on glass which could be tinted with dry colours and varnished or treated with transparent oil-based colours, as were lantern slides and stereoscopic slides. Results were often of poor quality, and an expert slide-maker pointed out that the "colours used are, as a rule, far too vivid, glaring, crude and bright, such as a Prussian blue sky with crimson-lake clouds. Not only is the wrong crude colour used, but far too much is put on. Remember that a fine stroke no thicker than a hair will come out like a branch of a tree on the screen. 'Near enough' will not do for lantern slide colouring!"

Albumen-coated surfaces provided a better ground for colours. Positives could be made on sensitized albumen on glass or paper and these proved suitable for colouring with oil paints, so that artists – even amateur ones – were able to produce finely coloured portraits, since the basic image was all there, the colour adding a certain realistic effect. Victorian photographers were aware of the shortcomings, as they saw them, of the black and white image. "The amateur photographer," said one advertisement, "must always deplore the fact that his best results with the Camera are poor reproductions of the scenes they represent. They lack the essential feature – NATURE'S COLOURING."

Victorian commercial studios were equipped to offer a service for hand-coloured photographs in water colours or in oils. When bromide printing papers came into general use in the 1870s, colours were often applied by tinting through stencils cut out for each colour, a similar technique to the airbrush masking methods of today. Results tended to be rather crude, as colours were sold ready-mixed for "Lips", "Flesh (dark or light)" or "Complexion"; or for landscape pictures using "Horizon", "Distance", "Leaves" and so on.

By the turn of the century most studios had a "While-U-Wait" hand-tinting service, as hand-colouring had become very popular. Purists objected, however, the photographers saying that it wasn't photography, the artists complaining that it wasn't art. Even so, the possibilities were exploited by both artists and photographers, and during the 1920s the surrealist artists and photographers such as Man Ray and Georges Hugnet experimented with hand-tinted photo-collages, while the German photographer Hans Bellmer produced coloured prints of the dolls he had made, arranged in provocative poses.

Today the process has come full circle, and hand-colouring is again a fashionable by-product of photography, with such exponents as the American painter-photographer Thomas Barrow; Harry Bowers; and Judith Golden, who colours with pastels and crayons. Many newly graduated photographers are experimenting with colours, some finding a deliberate, miniaturist approach successful, others opting for an impressionistic style, using marker pens to give a bold, sketchy effect that can be quite powerful.

THE WORK OF JAMES WEDGE

James Wedge is perhaps the first, or certainly one of the first photographers to pioneer the art of hand-colouring in modern commercial photography. His impressive output has inspired others to profit from his example and develop techniques of their own, photographers such as Bob Carlos Clarke and Andreas Huyman adding their own personal touch and guiding the genre in new directions. Wedge, one of our leading fashion photographers and a keen colourist, began tinting his own prints when, at the start of his career, he realised the need for a different approach to commercial photography, and began experimenting to find a fresh imagery. One of his first efforts, for the Sunday Times magazine, was a shot of stockings, in which he added a mechanical Letratone tint to the stockings, leaving the surrounding area in monochrome, an effect that made the colour sing vibrantly out.

The advantage of the hand-coloured print over the print made from colour negative film, is that your colouring can be selective, unique, and deliberately restricted, allowing you to pitch a single colour against a neutral background, or to distort colours for effect. This, of course, is the main benefit of the technique, since every print is virtually a "one-off" picture, and like a watercolour painting is the result of one person's interpretation. Thus, no two prints are ever exactly alike. With hand-tinting you have complete control over the final image, over the amount of colour, and choice of colour. That, as Wedge points out, "is the joy of it, throwing open a whole new creative area in photography."

A UNIQUE CONTRIBUTION

The hand-coloured print is no longer the poor relation of the full-colour photograph, but stands on its own, making a definite contribution to the photographer's gallery of original works. Furthermore, tinted prints – and this is an important point – have the decided advantage of being cheaper to produce than colour prints, once you have invested in colour dyes and brushes. It isn't even necessary to colour your own processed pictures – you could begin by practising on old black and white photographs, or picture postcards.

When you become more experienced, you can prepare your darkroom prints specially for tinting, by selectively lightening dark areas, by masking or dodging, or even by chemical bleaching. It is better to have a print without too many dark areas of tone (colour will really only be effective on the highlights, when gradations of tone and form show through thinly applied tints) and with a matt or semi-matt surface.

One of the most important points about hand-colouring is that it can take time. Careful preparation is half the battle, and the preliminary groundwork of masking can often take longer than the actual colouring process – James Wedge often takes a week or more to produce the desired effect. This means judiciously applying colours in transparent layers, using several different colours to create the desired jewel-like quality. Some photographers have become so expert in applying dyes with an aim to realism that it is hard to tell a hand-coloured print from a print made with a colour-film negative, except that the photographer has been able to give emphasis to selected areas of the image, or to intensify colour, in a way that the camera and film could not possibly achieve.

FASHION

Captions to the photographs in this section appear after Plate 32.

PLATE 1

PLATE 2

PLATE 3

PLATE 4

PLATE 5

PLATE 6

PLATE 7

PLATE 8

PLATE 9

PLATE 10

PLATE 11

PLATE 12

PLATE 13

PLATE 14

PLATE 15

PLATE 16

PLATE 17

PLATE 18

PLATE 19

PLATE 20

PLATE 21

PLATE 22

PLATE 23

PLATE 24

PLATE 25

PLATE 26

PLATE 27

PLATE 28

PLATE 29

PLATE 30

PLATE 31

PLATE 32

PLATE 1
This swimwear shot for *Honey* magazine
was meant to recall the transfer-type pin-ups
that are sometimes stuck to the sides of trucks.

Camera Contax	
Lighting Studio flash	
Film Tri-X	
Print Bromide	
Colour application Airbrush and paintbrush	

PLATES 2–5
I was asked to shoot these clown-like clothes for
19 Magazine. I wanted to give the pictures a
traditional clown feel without shooting them at an
obvious location, such as a circus. I decided to
shoot them in an old empty warehouse near my
studio which had textured walls, a wooden floor
and an old table. I dressed the set by putting old
make-up jars on the table, and pinned pictures
from Fellini's book on clowns on the walls.
Since I did not want the background to be too
predominant, hand-colouring suited the job well.
Plate 2 was shot with a canvas hung between two
walls. All of the pictures used the available light
entering the warehouse windows.

Camera Contax	
Lighting Daylight	
Print Bromide (sepia)	
Colour application Airbrush and paintbrush	

PLATES 6–9
These fashion pictures for *Cosmopolitan* were
influenced by the costume designer Bakst who
designed for the Ballets Russes. I took a lot of
trouble to find a model with the right looks who
could ballet dance, and happily the girl I chose
proved to be perfect. I shot in the studio on a
wooden floor with flash lighting positioned close
to the ground to give a theatrical mood.

Camera Contax	
Lighting Studio flash	
Film Tri-X	
Print Bromide print (sepia)	
Colour application Airbrush and paintbrush	

PLATES 10–13
For these swimwear pictures for *19* magazine I
wanted to create strong images but not at the cost
of sacrificing the clothes, which were the whole
reason for taking the pictures. I photographed the
model in my studio against a roughly painted wall.
During the printing stage I solarized the image.
To solarize a print you switch on the darkroom
lights for a second or two while the print is still in
the developer. You then finish developing, and fix
and wash in the normal way. This is a technique
said to have originated with the surrealist painter
and photographer Man Ray. While my image was
being solarized, I held a mask over the swimsuit
so that part of the print was unaffected. I then
hand-coloured the swimsuits in the same colours
as the originals.

Camera Contax	
Lighting Studio flash	
Film Tri-X	
Print Bromide print (solarized)	
Colour application Airbrush and paintbrush	

PLATES 14–16
In these lingerie pictures for *Cosmopolitan*, the
idea was to try to recreate the Vargas pin-up girl,
so hand-colouring suited the job perfectly. All the
shots were taken in my studio and then printed on
Kodak lith film to give a hard sharp image. I used
the airbrush to mould the body in a pin-up style.
After completing the hand-colouring, I sprayed
the back of the lith film with white car paint which
eliminated the transparency of the image.

Camera Hasselblad	
Lighting Flash	
Film Pan F	
Print Lith (sepia)	
Colour application Airbrush	

Plate 17

For this swimwear picture I wanted the girl to stand in water, but the aim was to produce a graphic, rather than realistic image. I photographed the model in my studio and then took a journey to the coast and made a picture of the sea. Two prints were made. The sea image was printed on bromide paper, vignetted so that just a small area of water was visible and this I toned blue. The picture of the girl was printed on Kodak lith film and toned sepia. I hand-coloured the lith print of the girl and then attached it to the bromide print of the sea.

Camera Contax	
Film Tri-X	
Print Bromide (blued toned); lith (sepia)	
Colour application Airbrush	

Plates 18 and 19

I was asked by *19* magazine to photograph this underwear in a style reminiscent of Victorian images, so hand-tinting suited these pictures perfectly. I built a small room set in the corner of my studio to give a Victorian feeling to the picture. Vignetting the print in the darkroom (holding back the corners of the picture under the enlarger by means of a circular mask or with my hands) added to the Victorian look. Plate 18 took a particularly long time to colour as the wallpaper was coloured following the pattern – each flower had to be the same colour throughout the print. Hand colouring is a slow painstaking job and unless you have patience, forget it!

Camera Hasselblad
Lighting Studio flash
Film Tri-X
Print Bromide (sepia, lightly dyed in bath of parchment-coloured shirt dye)
Colour application Airbrush and paintbrush

Plates 20–25

These theatrical clothes were photographed for *19* magazine. When I saw the clothes about a week before the shoot I immediately thought of Toulouse-Lautrec, and decided to photograph them with this painter in mind. Models with suitable looks were chosen and the hairdresser and make-up artist were briefed on the concept of the images. I then had to find a suitable location, and just in time for the shoot came across an old music hall in the East End of London which suited the pictures perfectly.

Camera Contax
Lighting Flash and theatre lights
Film Tri-X
Print Bromide (sepia)
Colour application Airbrush and paintbrush

Plate 26

This is a fashion picture for *Nova* magazine. It was intended to illustrate a fashion story on tights and body stockings that were being printed with pictures resembling tattoos. These tattoos would be printed on the thigh of a pair of tights or across the chest of a body stocking. I wanted my picture to maintain the image of the tattoo artist. I photographed the girl first and then the snake. I montaged the snake with the print of the girl so that it appeared to wrap around the body. I then tinted the design on the tights the same as the original and painted the snake with the same colours.

Camera Hasselblad
Film Plus-X
Lighting Studio flash
Print Bromide
Colour application Airbrush and paintbrush

PLATE 27

On this assignment my hand-colouring skills saved the day. I was photographing a crochet pattern of a dress that readers could send for and knit at home, for the *Mirror* magazine. Unfortunately the sample dress had been hanging around for some days, and when the model tried it on, it had stretched so badly that it looked terrible on her. The fashion editor tried pinning and bulldog clipping it but this made it worse. We had to produce a picture and there was no time to make a new dress, so I photographed the model nude and painted the dress on to the print with poster paints – and no-one was the wiser.

Camera Hasselblad	
Lighting Studio flash	
Film Tri-X	
Print Bromide (sepia)	
Colour application Paintbrush	

PLATES 28–31

I have a small cottage in the Forest of Dean in Gloucestershire and it was there that I shot these pictures for *19* magazine. It was springtime and I wanted the pictures to have the soft colours that are typical of the area. The clothes had very little colour in them, which was good for the country feeling I wanted to achieve. After producing the bromide prints, I sepia-toned them and then dyed them a warm beige using cold-water shirt dyes. I applied the colour mostly with cotton wool while the prints were damp, to keep the background colours soft. I used a paintbrush for the finer, sharper areas in the foreground.

Camera Contax	
Lighting Daylight	
Film Tri-X	
Print Bromide (dyed and sepia)	
Colour application Cotton wool and paintbrush	

PLATE 32

Photographed for *Honey* magazine, this is part of a series of pictures, but unfortunately this is the only one that has survived the years. I had intended to shoot these pictures on Piccadilly Circus. Although the model was very happy to do this, the fashion editor got cold feet at the last minute, so we shot them in my studio.

Camera Contax	
Film Tri-X	
Lighting Studio flash	
Print Bromide	
Colour application Airbrush	

BEAUTY

*Captions to the photographs in this section
appear after Plate 44.*

PLATE 33

PLATE 34

PLATE 35

PLATE 36

PLATE 37

PLATE 38

PLATE 39

PLATE 40

PLATE 41

PLATE 42

PLATE 43

PLATE 44

Plate 33

I took this picture for my wife Amanda, who is a make-up artist. She needed a beauty picture for a calendar her agent was producing. I wanted to keep the picture very simple, to show off Amanda's make-up to the full. I used a black bin liner wrapped around the model's head to help emphasize her face. During development I solarized the print, masking the face so that it would remain normal. I tinted the parts of the face where colour had been applied.

Camera Hasselblad	
Film Tri-X	
Print Bromide, part solarized	
Colour application Paintbrush and airbrush	

Plate 34

This beauty picture for *Marie Claire* magazine was shot to illustrate how make-up can hide many skin blemishes. I photographed the model without any make-up and this did indeed show up all the small blemishes which her make-up would normally hide. I made two bromide prints exactly the same size. One I left untouched, the other I hand-coloured as if she were made-up. I then collaged the two prints together.

Camera Hasselblad	
Lighting Studio flash	
Film Plus-X	
Print Bromide	
Colour application Airbrush and paintbrush	

Plate 35

There are many ways to make yourself appear suntanned without lying in the sun, and this picture for *She* magazine was intended to illustrate this. I made a bromide print and masked off half of the girl's body with liquid strip mask. I then sepia-toned the exposed area. I removed the strip mask and finished the picture by hand-colouring.

Camera Hasselblad	
Lighting Studio flash	
Film Plus-X	
Print Bromide (half sepia)	
Colour application Airbrush and paintbrush	

Plate 36

This is an experimental image showing a range of cosmetics in one picture. It consists of one photograph showing parts of the girl's face reflected from pieces of mirror. The girl faced a board with about eight small mirrors attached to it and angled to reflect parts of her face in each mirror. There was a piece of black felt hanging behind the model so that only her face was reflected. I painted a different lip or eye colour on each reflection.

Camera Contax	
Film Tri-X	
Lighting Studio flash	
Print Bromide	
Colour application Airbrush	

Plates 37 and 38

On these two beauty pictures I added colour using mixed media. For the image of the girl in the hat, (plate 37) I coloured her face and then covered that part of the print with a chenille face veil. For the girl with the scarf (plate 38) I sepia toned the print, hand-coloured the face, and then put a chiffon scarf around her neck, leaving one end hanging. I then put the print on a wall with a wind machine underneath. As the wind blew the chiffon across her face I copied the image using colour film.

Camera Contax	
Lighting Studio flash	
Film Tri-X and EPR	
Print Bromide (sepia and black and white)	
Colour application Airbrush, paintbrush and collaged fabric	

PLATES 39 AND 40
Early on in my career I was asked to do a cover for *Harpers & Queen*. Wanting to do something different from their usual straight colour covers, I decided to do a hand-coloured image. They chose plate 40. My first magazine cover.

Camera Hasselblad	
Lighting Studio flash	

PLATE 41
This beauty photograph was shot in the studio with flash lighting.

Camera Contax	
Lighting Studio flash	
Film Tri-X	
Print Bromide (sepia)	
Colour application Airbrush and paintbrush	

PLATE 42
For this beauty photograph for *19* magazine I took two separate black and white pictures of the girl's head and the flower using the same light source on each and the same camera angle. I then montaged the two images together and hand-coloured the result. I used the same colours for both the girl's hair and the petals of the flower, to unite them even more together; the girl's make-up was also coloured in harmonious tones.

Camera Hasselblad	
Film Plus-X	
Print Bromide	
Colour application Airbrush and paintbrush	

PLATE 43
I was asked by *19* magazine to create an image to go with an article on face cleansers. I photographed the girl against a white background and used studio flash for the lighting. After making my best print, I masked off part of the image with masking fluid in a way that looked as if the model had smeared it with her hand. I then sprayed solid white poster paint over the whole print. When this was dry, I peeled off the mask and coloured the girl's face underneath. The effect was an interesting image that also fitted the brief.

Camera Contax	
Film Tri-X	
Print Bromide (sepia)	
Colour application Airbrush	

PLATE 44
This beauty picture was made for *19* magazine to illustrate skin care. I decided to create a picture of a girl casting off her old, tired skin like a snake; from inside the old skin comes a beautiful tanned and flawless new body. I photographed the model, posing her in snake-like positions and lighting her body to complement the pose. I made two identical bromide prints; I sepia toned one and left the other black and white. I worked on the sepia print a little more with the airbrush. I stuck the black and white print over the coloured one and then simply peeled the black and white print off the upper part of the body.

Camera Contax	
Lighting Studio flash	
Film Tri-X	
Colour application Airbrush	

ADVERTISING

*Captions to the photographs in this section
appear after Plate 61.*

PLATE 45

PLATE 46

PLATE 47

PLATE 48

PLATE 49

PLATE 50

PLATE 51

PLATE 52

PLATE 53

PLATE 54

PLATE 55

PLATE 56

PLATE 57

PLATE 58

PLATE 59

PLATE 60

PLATE 61

PLATE 45

I was asked to produce an image of a girl recalling a sultry 1940s movie star holding a packet of Planters Peanuts; the colour was also to be reminiscent of that period. The advertisement was meant to suggest an old film poster, with copy that said 'She fell victim to the dry subtle spice' and 'Temptation beyond endurance'. I suggested to the art director that the best way to achieve the film poster effect for this period was to hand-colour it, and this was agreed, on the understanding that the colour of the product would remain the same as the original. I shot the picture in my studio using tungsten lighting that was as close as I could get to the lighting of those old movie days.

Camera Contax	
Lighting Tungsten	
Film Pan-F	
Print Bromide (sepia)	
Colour application Airbrush and paintbrush	

PLATES 46–47

These images were created to advertise gold. I had to photograph the girls from quite close, so that the jewellery would not appear too small. But I did not want the models to look too static, which can easily happen when you come in close on a face. So I used a wind machine and kept the girls moving all the time. I find gold the hardest colour of all to tint. It is a mistake simply to colour the jewellery yellow, because gold reflects so many different colours. I usually sart by colouring some areas green and then some blue, giving an overall wash of yellow and a little orange on some parts to finish. To make the gold look strong I kept the rest of the prints black and white, except for the very pale make-up colours. I printed the images on Kodak Precision Line film and after colouring I sprayed the back of the film with white car paint.

Camera Contax	
Film Tri-X	
Print On Kodak Precision Line film	
Colour application Airbrush and paintbrush	

PLATES 48, 49 AND 58

I was commissioned to do these shots by Wella Hair Products, who specifically wanted them hand-coloured. They had the finished work printed by a fine-art printer in an edition of 200 on very good art paper. I then signed the prints and they were given to Wella's best clients. It was rewarding to see my work printed so well.

Camera Contax	
Film Tri-X	
Print Bromide	
Colour application Airbrush	

PLATE 50

When I was asked to shoot this advertisement for Colman's Mustard the company was running a series of rather bizarre images with the copy line 'C'mon Colman's, light my fire'. My picture was to look like a Victorian sea-side post card incorporating a giant-sized pot of mustard. Hand-colouring suited this concept well. The set was built in my studio with a painted canvas backdrop and sand on the floor. A Punch and Judy booth was set up and two dwarfs were hired to play the characters handing each other the large replica pot of Colman's Mustard.

Camera Gandolfi 5×4	
Film Plus-X	
Print Bromide (sepia)	
Colour application Airbrush, paintbrush and cotton wool	

PLATES 51 AND 52

These advertisements were the most difficult I have undertaken, the hardest part being the product. The wine had to be the exact pink colour, and the label on the bottle also had to be coloured realistically. For this I worked with my finest brush and a magnifying glass.

Camera Contax	
Film Plus-X	
Print Bromide	
Colour application Airbrush, paintbrush and cotton wool	

PLATES 53–56
I have been working on the Russell and Bromley
advertisements for many years, always shooting
in straight colour. On this occasion I suggested to
my client that I should photograph a naked girl,
not wearing the shoe, and hand-tint the result.
This came as a shock to my client as in the past
the model had always worn beautiful clothes, with
shoes on, and the images were in straight colour.
It took some persuasion, but he finally agreed.

Camera Contax	
Print Bromide (blue-toned)	
Colour application Airbrush	

PLATE 57
I was commissioned by Biba to photograph this
nude lying on a pile of cushions. The idea was to
place the picture at a prime spot just outside
Heathrow Airport, with the copy saying 'Welcome
to Biba'. Unfortunately the poster was banned by
the authorities as they said it was liable to cause
road accidents. So, as far as I know, it was never
used.

Camera Contax	
Lighting Studio flash	
Print Bromide	
Colour application Airbrush and paintbrush	

PLATE 59
This is one of my favourite beauty pictures. It was
an advertisement for Christie face products. This
is one of two pictures that I produced for the
campaign. The other head shot (a girl's head in a
space helmet) I liked equally well, and in fact it
won an award. Unfortunately, because of time and
my filing system, this image has been lost, and as
hand-coloured pictures can never be reproduced
exactly the same, it is one of many pictures I am
unable to show in this book.

Camera Contax	
Lighting Studio flash	
Film Tri-X	
Print Bromide (sepia)	
Colour application Airbrush and paintbrush	

PLATE 60
Mary Quant Cosmetics asked me to shoot a
moody picture of a girl in the country, rather than
a hard-sell image of the product. The softness of
the picture was achieved by applying the colours
on to a damp print, mostly with cotton wool.

Camera Contax	
Lighting Daylight	
Film Tri-X	
Colour application Cotton wool and paintbrush	

PLATE 61
I was asked by a client to produce a picture
that depicted eastern perfumes, to illustrate an
article that they were doing on the subject. This is
how the picture was achieved. First the model,
wearing a kimono, was shot surrounded by
flowers on my studio floor. The background was
black (very important) and the lighting was flash.
Next I searched London for a large round perfume
bottle and, having found one, I then searched
again for someone to cut it in half. After many
telephone calls and a lot of foot work, a person
was found who split the bottle in half from top to
bottom. Then in the darkroom I printed my
oriental girl with the half bottle on the bromide
paper and a flower stuck in the top. The image of
the girl was then exposed through the bottle and
developed in the normal way. The result was a
slightly softer image of the girl surrounded by the
white replica of the bottle and flower. This type of
result is known as a rayograph, after Man Ray,
who is said to have discovered the technique. I
finally hand-coloured the print.

Camera Hasselblad	
Lighting Studio flash	
Film Plus-X	
Print Bromide (sepia)	
Colour application Airbrush and paintbrush	

INTERIORS

*Captions to the photographs in this section
appear after Plate 71.*

PLATE 62

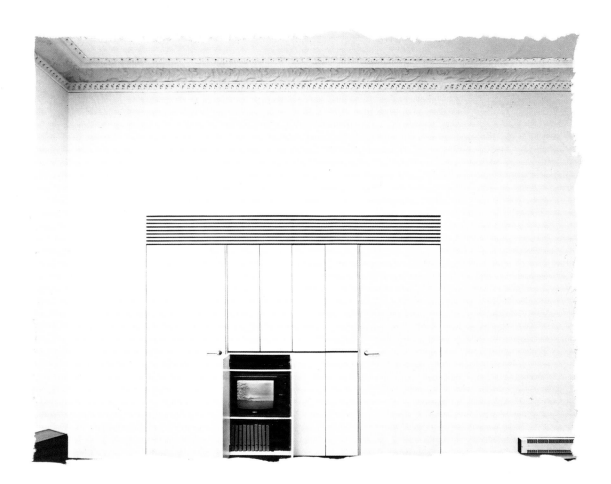

PLATE 63

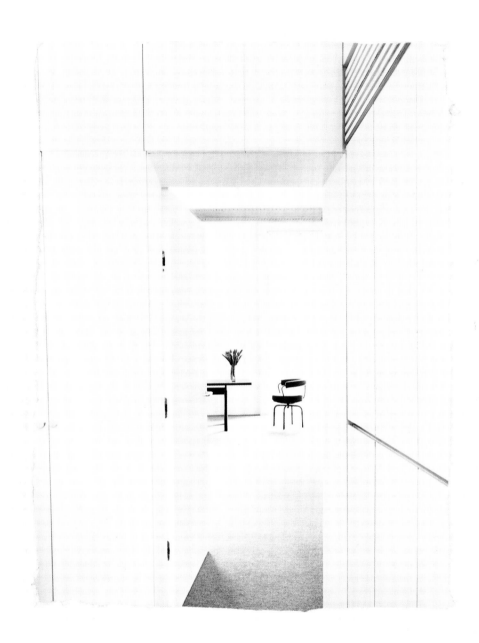

PLATE 64

PERSONAL IMAGES

Captions to the photographs in this section
appear after Plate 71.

PLATE 65

PLATE 66

PLATE 67

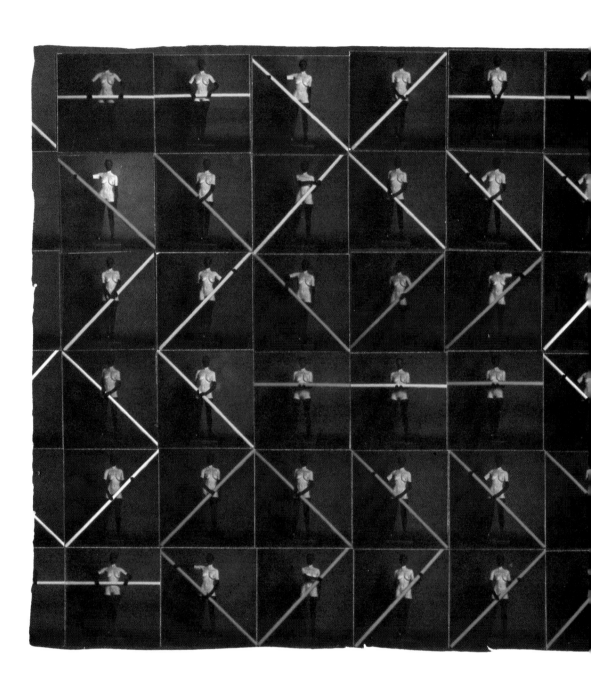

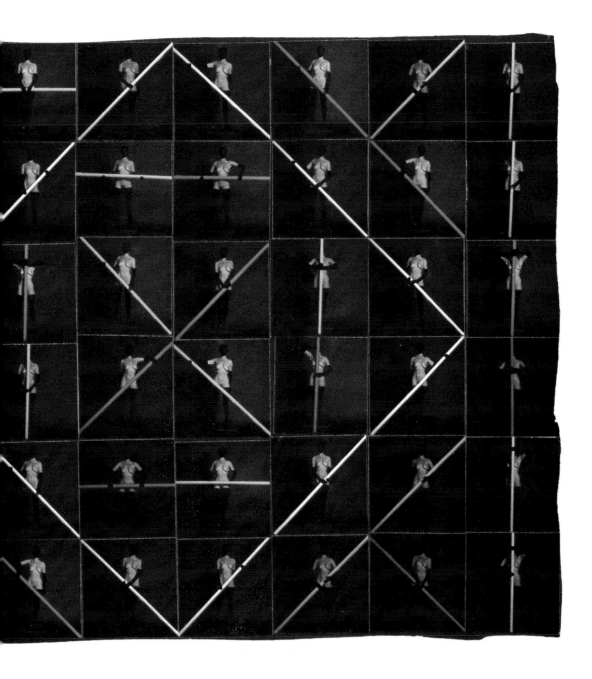

PLATE 68

PLATE 69

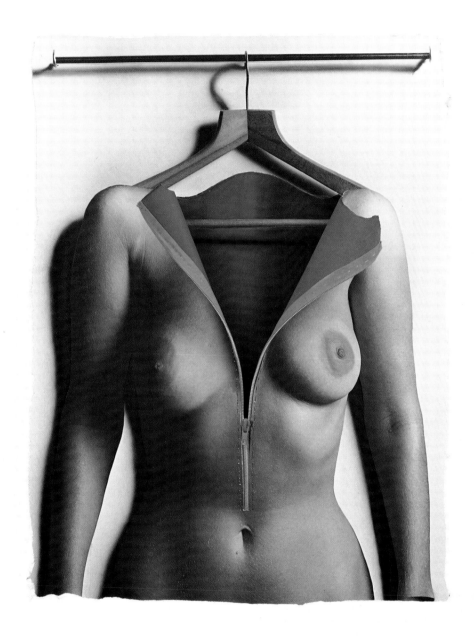

PLATE 70

PLATE 71

PLATES 62–64

I have undertaken many assignments for an excellent magazine called *Interiors*, but have only once found the need to produce a hand-coloured series. The flat, owned and designed by architect John Pawson, had no armchairs, no beds, no paintings, no objects. Minimalism was a generous term for it. Colour was so scarce in this environment ('an iceberg', as the magazine called it) that it seemed ideal for the hand-tinting technique. The kitchen (plate 62) had no colour in it at all, so I placed the piece of meat on the chrome table top to give me something to tint. In the other rooms I coloured the cornice the pink that it was, the television screen, and the flowers. I am pleased to say that I won an award for this assignment.

Camera Gandolfi 5×4

Lighting Daylight and flash

Film Plus-X

Print Bromide

Colour application Airbrush and paintbrush

PLATE 65

Camera Contax

Lighting Studio flash

Print Bromide

Colour application Airbrush

PLATES 66–67

Camera Hasselblad

Lighting Studio flash

Print Bromide

Colour application Collage

PLATE 68

Camera Hasselblad

Lighting Studio flash

Print Bromide

Colour application Paintbrush

PLATE 69

Camera Contax

Lighting Studio flash

Print Bromide

Colour application Collage

PLATE 70

Camera Contax

Lighting Studio flash

Print Bromide (sepia toned)

Colour application Airbrush and collage

PLATE 71

Camera Hasselblad

Lighting Studio flash

Print Kodak Line Film

Colour application Airbrush

Hand-colouring *Techniques*

WHY HAND-COLOUR?

Until comparatively recently, hand-colouring black and white prints was the most reliable way of obtaining a colour photographic image. During the nineteenth and early twentieth centuries there were numerous attempts at creating a colour photographic process and some, such as the autochrome process, gained a significant following. But none of these early processes produced a lifelike enough result to supply popular demand, and most professional photographic studios employed at least one hand-colourist until the time of the first world war, in some cases until later still.

Today's fast, reliable colour films have changed this state of affairs. With realistic colour available to every photographer, hand-colouring has developed into an art form in its own right, and the technique is used extensively—particularly in advertising photography, where precise control over the final image is of paramount importance.

The uses of hand-colouring in advertising photography are varied and extensive. The technique allows a product or garment to be emphasized in the picture so that the viewer's attention is drawn to it immediately. Hand-colouring is also used widely in beauty photography, where lips, skin, and eyes can all be tinted.

Photographers who hand-colour their work now do so for a variety of reasons. I began hand-colouring because of the close control the technique could give me over the colour of the image; it also allowed me to bring a new and personal interpretation to many of my subjects—particularly in fashion and beauty work. I value hand-colouring for the way it allows selective colouring, with some areas of a print in black and white, some in colour; for the way hand-colouring can be used to influence the mood of a picture; for its potential for surrealistic effects, and so on. Hand-colouring is also attractive to many people because it is one of the ways in which a reproducible photograph can be turned into a unique work of art.

PICTURES FOR COLOURING

Which images the photographer chooses for hand-colouring is very much a matter for personal preference. Photographic dyes work best when applied to light or mid-range tones, however, and it is generally best to go for lighter-than-average prints. If there is an area in a print that is particularly dark, it is usually preferable to leave this untoned.

ABOVE From the early years of photography until quite recently, hand-tinting was the only method of applying realistic colour to an image. Pictures like this were popular in the Victorian and Edwardian periods.

Film choice is also up to the individual. I like to use grain as a dominant visual element in my pictures and so I generally use Kodak Tri-X, rated normally at 400 ISO, to give a grainy effect.

You can use photographs taken with any of the light sources you would normally use, although you should bear in mind that daylight often gives a softer image than flash.

It is useful to have some knowledge of camera filters and their effect on the black and white image. I often use yellow, orange or red filters to darken the sky and emphasize the clouds. When shooting beauty images I frequently use a red filter, so that the lips do not print too dark. If the model has red lips, these can often appear dark grey or even black on a black and white print. This means that any red colour that you want to add is lost because the dark tones come through.

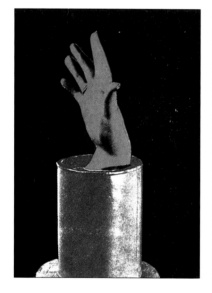

ABOVE Bizarre as well as naturalistic effects are possible with hand-colouring.

RIGHT To give a good basis for hand-colouring areas such as the lips, the tone should be light in the original image. Bright red lipstick is unsuitable because it will look dark in a black and white print.

PROCESSING THE FILM

Before you start to process any film, you should make sure that everything in your darkroom is clean, neat, and tidy. Arrange your equipment into wet and dry areas, with all your chemicals, tanks, trays, and print washers on the wet side, your enlarger, mounting equipment, and all the other items you use before and after working with the chemicals, on the dry side. Keep everything in its place in this way, and stick to a regular routine, and you will work more easily and efficiently in the dark.

LOADING THE FILM

One particular technique that you should practise before you begin is loading film on to reels before inserting these into the developing tank. Try this with old film in daylight first, and make sure that you thread the film on to the reel without it buckling – there is nothing more frustrating than having a kink mark on a frame you want to print. Plastic tanks are easier for the beginner and have the added advantage of adjusting to different film formats. Metal tanks are less easy to load, but easier to keep dry and clean.

WORKING IN DAYLIGHT

After you have loaded the film tank, the film is protected from fogging, so you can work in daylight. There are four main stages: development (which turns the latent image on the film into a visible image); stop bath (which arrests the action of the developer); fixing (which makes the images permanent and renders invisible the excess chemicals used in development); and washing (which allows you to clear away the unused chemicals from the film).

At each stage it is important to work carefully and consistently. You can control the development process in a number of ways (by the temperature of your chemicals, by the amount of time you develop the film, and by the degree of agitation you apply to the film tank), so it is important to follow the instructions carefully if you want good and reliable results.

PROCESSING EQUIPMENT
There is a bewildering variety of equipment available for all aspects of darkroom work. The list below contains the basic essentials for film processing. In addition it is worth considering a tempering box to keep all your tanks and solutions at the right temperature, a water filter, and a film dryer.

- Daylight developing tank and reels
- Bottles – for developing solutions
- Measuring cylinder and funnel – for pouring out solutions accurately
- Photographic thermometer
- Darkroom timer that gives an audible signal when the time set has elapsed
- Rubber hose
- Film clips
- Scissors

PROCESSING PROCEDURE

1 Fill a measuring cylinder with 32 fl oz (1 l) of water at 70°F (21°C). Then pour 1 fl oz (30 ml) each of solutions B and C into the cylinder.

2 In the dark, load the film on to reels, taking care not to buckle it, especially if it is 120 format. Pre-soak the film in water for 2 to 3 min. Then add 3 fl oz (90 ml) of solution A to the measuring jug.

3 Pour away the pre-soaking water, add the developer to the tank, and agitate for 30 sec by inverting the tank. Then agitate 4 or 5 times every 30 sec. Develop Tri-X film for 19 min, HP4 for 14 min.

4 Pour away the spent developer and wash the film in stop bath for 1 min. Then add the fixer, mixed 1:9 with water at 70°F (21°C). To establish the fixing time, put a small amount of exposed film into the fixer and time how long it takes for the film to become clear. Multiply this time by three to give the fixing time.

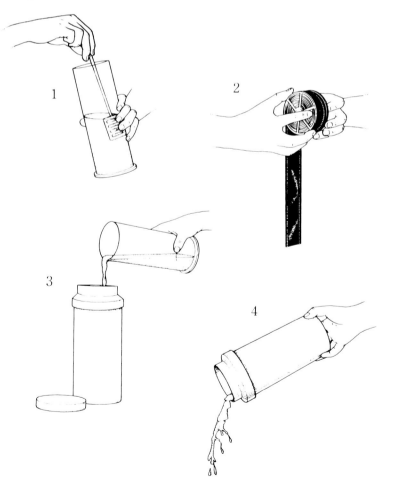

5 Connect a hose to the tank reel and wash the film continuously in water for 20 to 30 min. It is worthwhile fixing a filter to the water supply to prevent particles of dirt becoming embedded in the emulsion.

6 Add two drops of wetting solution to the water. This reduces the surface tension of the water, to improve draining, speed up drying, and reduce the risk of drying marks on the surface of the film.

7 After carefully removing the developed film from the spiral, wipe it down with a very soft chamois leather. Hold the film securely at the top and pull the chamois leather down gently but firmly.

8 Put the film into a pre-warmed drying cabinet. After it is dry you can cut it into strips for contact printing before putting it into clear negative sleeves.

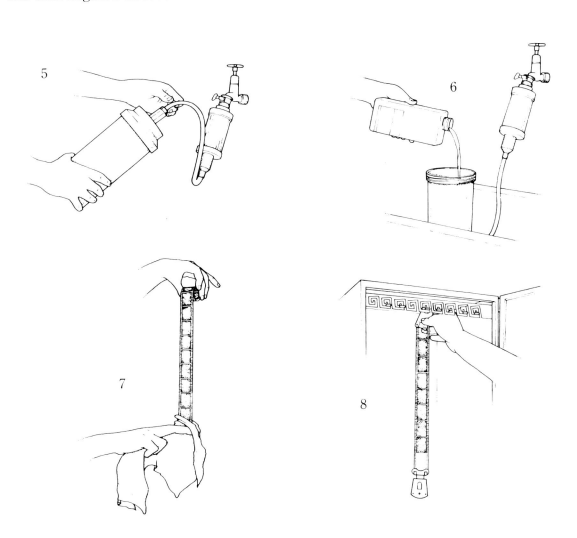

PRINTING

EQUIPMENT FOR PRINTING
- Enlarger
- Masking frame—to hold the printing paper flat on the enlarger baseboard
- Printing paper
- Orange safelight
- Cardboard shapes attached to lengths of stiff wire—for burning and dodging
- Darkroom timer
- Containers for chemicals
- Trays for chemicals— allocate trays to particular chemicals, to lessen the risk of contamination
- Measuring cylinders—for mixing developer, stop bath and fixer
- Darkroom thermometer
- Print tongs
- Print washer

Before printing any negative, you should spend some time thinking about the qualities you will want in the end result. The degree of contrast you will require, whether you intend to tone the print before hand-colouring, and whether you are going to solarise the print before colouring—all these factors should influence your choice of chemicals and papers. You should use a matte or semi-matte paper for hand-colouring. If I am going to sepia-tone or blue-tone a print I use Ilford Gallery paper, because it holds the toner evenly and keeps the highlights clean. When solarising a print I find that I usually obtain the best results on Agfa Record Rapid paper. For a print that I am not going to pre-tone, I normally use either Agfa Portriga or Agfa Brovira papers.

PRINTING TECHNIQUES

Producing a print involves two main stages, both of which should be done under safelighting. First you expose the print in the enlarger; then you process it in developing chemicals. The developing stage involves a sequence of chemicals similar to those used for processing a film (developer, stop bath, fixer, and wash), but the development is carried out in trays rather than in light-tight tanks.

When printing, you should be prepared to use several sheets of paper before you get a result of the correct standard. This is not just because you may want to make test strips to try different exposure times, but also because you will probably need to alter the exposure locally on different parts of the print. You do this by "dodging and burning"—holding a specially shaped piece of black card over any area where you want to hold back exposure, while allowing the light to "burn in" on to the other parts of the print. This is obviously a process that calls for a great deal of experimenting in order to get it right.

CHOOSING PRINTS FOR COLOURING

When selecting a print for hand-colouring, you should look for different qualities from those you would normally expect in an ideal, well-produced print. Choose a light-toned print (you can leave any very dense black areas uncoloured) with plenty of detail for the best results.

The Printing Process

1 Before beginning, prepare your darkroom carefully. Select the negative you want to print and put it into the negative carrier; set out your chemicals; adjust your enlarger's masking frame to the right size; and switch on the safelight.

2 Carefully focus the image on the base of the masking frame. Then stop down the lens to your chosen setting. Put a sheet of paper in the masking frame and expose the paper. Hold back any areas you want to lighten by dodging—keep the wire moving all the time.

3 Develop the print for at least 2 min—full development is essential for an evenly toned print. Put the print face down into the stop bath and keep it there for 10–15 sec. Remove the print from the stop bath and put it into the first tray of fixing solution. Follow this with a second fix in clean solution. Remove any traces of fix from the print before washing by using hypo clearing agent. Wash the print for 30 min in running water, then dry it. You can use a frame stretched with muslin, and dry the print emulsion side down.

4 You can use ferricyanide solution to bleach out areas of the print that are too dark and will not take colour well. Apply the solution with a cotton wool bud.

NOTE: Two-stage developer
When using two-stage developer, place the print in the Amidol for 1½ min and then put it in Dektol. It will develop very rapidly, so you should keep it moving in the chemical to remove all the streak marks. Once the print has developed, use the same process as for the single-stage developer.

CHEMICALS FOR PRINTING

For a print that I am going to tone before hand-colouring, I use Dektol, mixed 1:1 with water at 70°F (21°C). Dektol is available as a powder and needs no preparation apart from mixing with the water. When hand-colouring a print without giving it a base tone I use Amidol for the first developer, and Dektol for the second developer. When using Dektol in this way I mix it 1:2.5 with water at 70°F (21°C). Whichever type of developer you are using, make sure that the Amidol or Dektol has completely dissolved. The formula for Amidol is as follows:

60 fl oz (1.75 l) water at 70°F (21°C)
2 oz (60 g) sodium sulfite
⅔ oz (20 g) Amidol
12 cc potassium bromide in 10% solution
12 cc citric acid in 10% solution

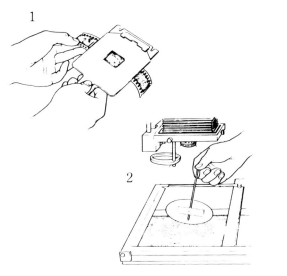

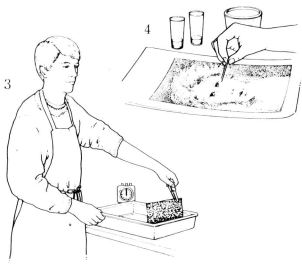

PREPARING THE PRINT

BLEACHING AND TONING CHEMICALS

Toning chemicals are commercially available in a range of colours. You can usually make up your own bleach solution using the following formula. This is for a stock solution, which you should dilute 1:9 in water before use.

1 oz (30 g) potassium
    bromide
1 oz (30 g) potassium
    ferricyanide
10 fl oz (300 ml) water

Before you begin to hand-colour a black and white print there are several preparatory techniques that you may need to carry out in order to get the best results.

Firstly there are two processes that can help make the image itself more suitable for hand-colouring. Bleaching the photograph removes any unwanted details and lightens the image; it also prepares the surface for the next process, toning. Toning the print completely or selectively with a colour such as sepia gives a warm background that will show off the colours to good advantage.

Secondly, you will need to prepare the photograph for the colouring process itself. You do this by mounting the picture, cleaning it with cotton wool soaked in lighter fuel, and masking it—covering up the areas that you do not want to colour.

BLEACHING AND TONING

For these techniques you work on a fully developed print in normal lighting. As well as the bleaching and toning chemicals and their trays, you will require a pair of rubber gloves to protect your hands.

When bleaching a print, you apply a solution of potassium ferricyanide and potassium bromide dissolved in water. The chemical effect of this is to change the black metallic silver that makes up the image into silver bromide. This produces a pale, straw-coloured image which will accept the toner.

Toning darkens the image once more, but in the colour of your chosen toner. I normally use either blue or sepia when toning photographs for hand-colouring, although many other colours are available.

MASKING

After you have mounted and cleaned the image, the last stage before applying the colour is to mask out selected areas. This is the most time-consuming technique in the whole process. There are several materials that you can use for masking, the most popular being sheets of clear plastic masking film and liquid masking solution. I prefer the latter, which can be painted on to any photographic surface and is easy to remove when it has set by attaching sticky tape and peeling off. Masking is particularly important when you are applying colour with an airbrush. For more information about masking, see the section on airbrushing, pages 110–111.

BLEACHING AND TONING PROCEDURE

1 Give the print a good soak in clean water for several minutes before blotting it to remove the surface moisture.

2 Working carefully, use a paintbrush to bleach around the edges of the area you are treating. Do not let the liquid run.

3 For larger areas, apply the bleach with a sponge. Small, clean artist's sponges are the easiest to use.

4 When you have applied bleach to the print, fix it and rinse it in clean water before toning.

5 Put the print into a tray of toner solution, agitating it gently. Remove and wash when the toner has stopped darkening.

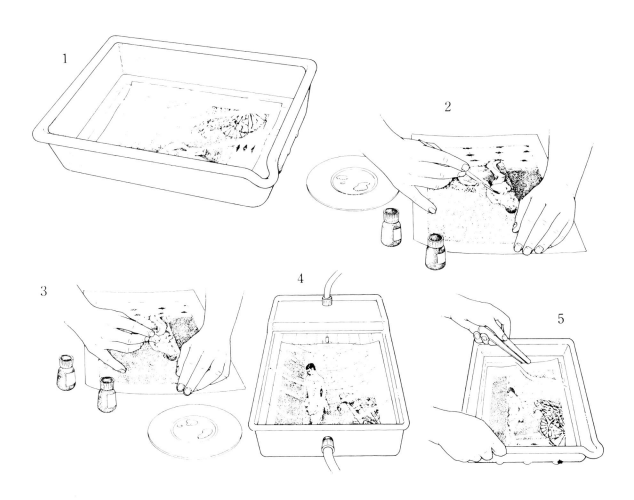

APPLYING THE COLOUR

There are many ways of colouring a correctly prepared print. You can use water-based colours, oil paints, felt-tipped pens and even coloured pencils and crayons. Indian inks give brilliant colours, opaque paints such as poster colour and gouache are useful when you do not want the image to show through, but the medium I use most is water-based photographic dye. This is easy to mix and gives soft, subtle colours.

One important advantage of this type of dye is that it produces a completely transparent colour that does not obscure the photographic quality of the print beneath. Water-based dyes are available in kit form from most large photographic retailers. A typical kit contains a range of about eight different colours. You can mix these colours together to form new colours and they can also be mixed with water to change their intensity and covering power. White is not normally included, but if this is required, you can use white ink. Suppliers of the dyes also provide a reducing agent that you can use for removing colour once it has been applied.

The strength of colour of the final result depends to a large extent on the density of the original black and white image—the lighter this is, the stronger the colours will be after treatment. This is why dodging during the printing process, to control the density of each area of the print, is so important.

APPLICATION TECHNIQUES

To assist in the even application of the dyes, it is a good idea to soak the print in clean, warm water for about 15 minutes before beginning to put on the colour. After this period, remove the print from the water, place it image-upwards on your work surface and soak up the excess moisture with a sheet of blotting paper. The surface should still be damp at this point, but do not worry about the dyes running on the damp surface—this will only happen if you apply too much colour at any one time.

There are three principal methods of applying the dye—with a brush, with cotton wool, or with an airbrush. Of these, the first two are best for beginners, since all you need to worry about is the colour, and not the technical skills involved in using an airbrush. Once you become proficient, however, you will be able to apply all three techniques to the same print, using the airbrush for the broad areas of colour, the conventional brush for small details, and the cotton wool for special textured or dappled effects.

Whichever method you use to apply the colour, there are two important principles that apply. Firstly, never try to achieve full-strength colour at one go. Instead, build up the effect slowly using thin washes of colour. After each application of colour, blot off any excess dye. Remember that the dyes are highly concentrated. If using a brush, for example, dip the tip into the colour and stir it into some plain water on a saucer or a small mixing dish. If you are happy with the colour, then, and only then, apply it to the print. If there is an area of the image that you want to remove, use an opaque medium, such as gouache or poster paint, rather than trying to cover it with successive layers of transparent dye.

Secondly, always start with the largest areas of the plainest colours. Once these are down on the print you can overlay them with progressively stronger concentrations of colour.

Applying Colour by Hand

A paintbrush is a particularly good tool with which to apply colour to all the small, fine areas of a print. Begin with a bleached and toned print which you have soaked in water for 15 minutes or so.

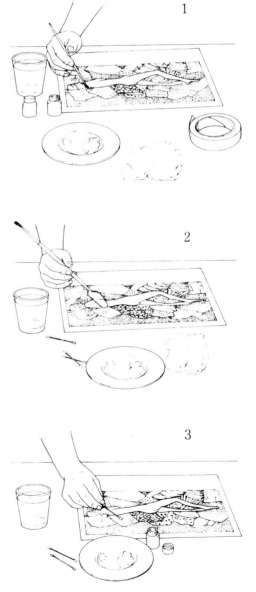

1 Use a sheet of blotting paper to remove excess water from the surface of the print. Add a tiny amount of concentrated dye to a container of water to produce the dilute mixture required. Start to spread the transparent colour on to the broader areas of the print, working with one of your larger brushes. Blot off any excess dye and build up the depth of the colour by applying more layers. Blot again if necessary. Use the same technique of building up layers on the areas of detail, but work with a smaller brush. Add any highlights and fine details using opaque colour on a small paintbrush.

2 Cotton wool is useful for soft areas of an image, such as delicate streaks of blue in a cloudy sky, or soft, distant trees or hills. The colour is applied by wiping over the area with cotton wool dipped in clean water and then, before it has dried, carefully blending in the colour. The action is repeated until you have reached the desired strength of colour. It is easier to use cotton wool if it is wrapped around the end of a paintbrush handle or a pencil and then used as a brush.

3 You can also apply colour using a cotton wool bud. This is particularly useful for smaller areas of the print.

AIRBRUSHING

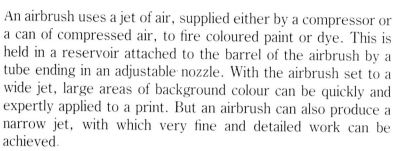

An airbrush uses a jet of air, supplied either by a compressor or a can of compressed air, to fire coloured paint or dye. This is held in a reservoir attached to the barrel of the airbrush by a tube ending in an adjustable nozzle. With the airbrush set to a wide jet, large areas of background colour can be quickly and expertly applied to a print. But an airbrush can also produce a narrow jet, with which very fine and detailed work can be achieved.

There are two main types of airbrush—single-action and double-action. The double-action type is much the best for detailed work. Its advantage is that it gives you full control over the flow of both paint and air through the airbrush, making it much easier to control the density of the colour.

Airbrushes also vary in the paint capacity of their reservoirs. I use two airbrushes: the first is the familiar pencil-shaped type that has a very small reservoir and is ideal for working on tiny details with small quantities of paint. The other has a large cup that takes much more paint and is better for broader areas.

USING AN AIRBRUSH

This seems difficult at first, but you will be surprised how much you can achieve with patience and practice. It is best to begin by experimenting on some clean paper or board before starting work on one of your prints. Practise airbrushing straight lines and, as you do so, try raising and lowering the brush so that the breadth of the line varies. Then attempt some simple shapes. To build up the desired strength of colour you should apply the dye in layers, just as you would if you were using a conventional brush or a piece of cotton wool. First try achieving an even density of colour, using regular strokes and keeping the airbrush the same distance from the paper as you move. Next practise vignetting the edges of your shapes by applying more layers of colour in the middle of the shape, and progressively fewer as you get nearer the edges. Once you have mastered these basic techniques you should be able to work quite quickly.

The time-consuming part of the airbrushing process involves making masks to protect the various areas of the print as you apply the different colours. There are several materials available from which you can make masks. One of the most popular is transparent self-adhesive masking film. This is used by covering the whole print and then progressively cutting and removing different areas as you colour different parts of the

AIRBRUSHING EQUIPMENT
○ Airbrush—there are many types on the market; choose a small-capacity pencil-type to start with
○ Masking solution—alternatively, you can use sheets of self-adhesive masking film
○ Masking tape
○ Photographic dyes
○ Scalpel and blades
○ Magnifying glass—for viewing fine details
○ Dishes—for mixing colours
○ Paintbrushes—use sable paintbrushes to load and clean the airbrush

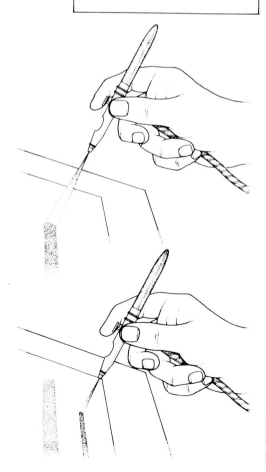

photograph. The difficulty here is using the scalpel with the correct amount of pressure—too much, and you go through the print, too little and you do not cut the film. I prefer a liquid masking solution which you can brush on, covering the exact area that you want to mask. When it has set you can airbrush the print in the normal way, removing the mask by peeling it off when the paint is dry.

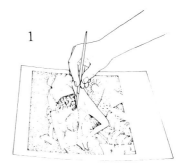

After masking, it is worth making some test strokes outside the border of the print to check that the airbrush is operating efficiently and that the colour is right. Then, when you have the correct rhythm, move on to the print proper, taking care not to overcolour.

When you have finished using one colour, you must clean the airbrush thoroughly before filling it with the next dye. Do this by getting rid of any surplus dye in the airbrush (remove most of it from the reservoir with a paintbrush, and spray the rest out). Then fill the airbrush with clean water and spray this through to wash out the reservoir and nozzle. Soak the airbrush in water with detergent added if it is still not clean. Finally, dry out the reservoir with a clean paintbrush.

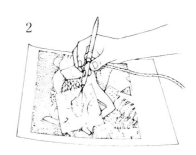

AIRBRUSHING PROCEDURE

1 Tape down your print and brush on the masking solution. Allow it to dry before starting to colour.

2 Fill the airbrush and start to spray. Control the air by pressing the button down. To release the dye, pull the control away from the jet. Spray evenly and do not put too much dye down in one go. Wash the airbrush thoroughly before adding further tones to the photograph.

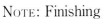

3 Leave the work to dry before removing the mask. A good way to take off the mask is to attach masking tape to the surface and peel this off. It will take the strip mask with it.

4 You can also remove the strip mask with your fingers.

NOTE: Finishing

After you have coloured your print and left it to dry, you should clean it throughly with cotton wool soaked in lighter fuel. Remember that your finished print is both delicate and unique. For storage or transport, cover it with sheets of tracing paper to protect it from damage. For display, mount it within a border of the appropriate colour. If you are going to display a large number of prints, consider dry mounting them. You can get them mounted professionally if you do not want to invest in costly dry-mounting equipment.

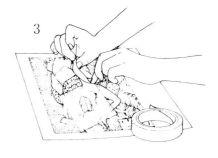

The Author

James Wedge began his photographic career in the
early 1970s, combining prestigious editorial and advertising work with
his own personal projects. He quickly built up an international
reputation particularly for his hand-coloured images, and has had
exhibitions of his work in London, New York, Milan and Amsterdam.
He has also lectured on photography in a number of art schools and
has published two other books, JAMES WEDGE PHOTOGRAPHY and
PRIVATE VIEWING.

Acknowledgements

The authors and publishers would like to thank the
following companies for permission to reproduce photographs in this
book: Russell and Bromley; Christie Cosmetics; Reckitt and Colman
Products Ltd; Smiths Crisps/Nabisco Group for pictures advertising
Planters peanuts (note: Planters is a registered trade mark;
Nabisco is the owner of the copyright for the Planters pack
and design).

Wella photographs reproduced by kind permission of
Wella Great Britain.

Mateus Rosé photograph reproduced by kind permission of Sogrape.